What the Night Keeps

Poems by M. J. Arcangelini

Stubborn Mule Press
Devil's Elbow, MO
stubbornmulepress.com

Copyright © Michael Joseph Arcangelini, 2019
First Edition 1 3 5 7 9 10 8 6 4 2
ISBN: 978-1-950380-39-8
LCCN: 2019942222

Design, edits and layout: Jeanette Powers
Cover image: Jon Lee Grafton
Title page image: M. J. Arcangelini
Author photo: Jeffrey Braverman
All rights reserved. No part of this publication may be reproduced or transmitted in any form or by any means, electronic or mechanical, including photocopying, recording or by info retrieval system, without prior written permission from the author.

Some of these poems previously appeared in the following magazines, anthologies, and websites (some in slightly different versions):

Hessler Street Fair Poetry Anthology - "Love Lies Bleeding," "Reinventing the Dead," "Crucifixions Are Boring," "I Should Fall In Love Again"
White Crane Journal - "Panhandled"
The Still Blue Project - "The Man Across the Street," "Impulse"
Love Jets: Queer Male Poets On 200 Years Of Walt Whitman - "Walt Whitman Poses for BEAR Magazine (1996)," "Walt Whitman Attends a Bear Weekend (2012) I: At the Pool"
Winedrunk Sidewalk: Shipwrecked In Trumpland - "The Political Climate Heats Up," "Stocks Open UP, " "To Be Heard"
The Gasconade Review – "Marcus Considers a Dog," "A Slow Collapse," "Air Quality Index"
After/Ashes: A Camp Fire Anthology – "Red Flags in November"
Antennae The Antennae – "The Finch"
The Beautiful Space: A Journal Of Mind, Art And Poetry – "Today, Tomorrow"

Thanks to Camden M. Collins for editorial suggestions on "In Orlando."

TABLE OF CONTENTS

Love Lies Bleeding / 1

Thin Walls / 2

The Occasional Unaccountable Urge to Clean House / 4

A Walk Through The Past / 5

To Be Heard / 6

A Few Weeks Before Xmas / 7

Panhandled / 8

Attitude Adjustment / 12

Pissing In the Sink / 13

The Man Across The Street / 15

Subverting the Sun / 18

The Balloons Are Back / 19

Insomnia / 20

Forest Dreams / 21

Her Breathing / 23

Another Suicide / 26

Grief / 27

Reminders / 28

Ghosts in the Mist / 30

Reinventing the Dead / 31

Walt Whitman Poses for BEAR Magazine (1996) / 33

Walt Whitman Attends a Bear Weekend (2012)

    I: At the Pool / 34

    II: Beyond the Bonfire / 36

Crucifixions Are Boring / 38

Loving Humanity / 39

Failure as an Adult / 41

The Rainbow Augury / 43

The Political Climate Heats Up / 45

Marcus Considers a Dog / 47

The Absence of Birds / 49

In December Woods / 50

A Slow Collapse / 51

Moonlight & Music / 53

The Belt / 54

Snap / 56

My Father's Post-Mortem Apology / 57

What the Night Keeps / 58

The Future / 60

Stocks Open Up / 61

The Norco Kicks In / 63

Quit: Day 11 / 64

Impulse / 65

Red Flags in November / 67

Air Quality Index / 69

Disaster Porn / 70

The Finch / 73

Poems Travel / 74

Clocks Don't Tick / 75

Independence Day, 2018 / 77

Today, Tomorrow / 79

The Cure for Depression / 80

After Emily Dickinson / 81

Used Book / 82

In Orlando / 83

The Lost Poem / 85

Parable of the End of Time / 86

I Should Fall in Love Again / 88

Nature Boy / 89

As a Child / 90

for Mikal Shively

LOVE LIES BLEEDING

Love lies bleeding on the gravel driveway
I thought I could do without it
so I beat it half to death,
following as it crawled across
the crunchy summer grass
beating it with a tire iron
telling it, through gritted teeth,
to go away and never come back
but it wouldn't get up and leave
so I had to keep beating it
calling it the dirty names of past lovers
I don't need you I said
I can grow old by myself
but it wouldn't leave so it had to be killed
now it lies bleeding in my gravel driveway
and when it has finally expired
the turkey buzzards will come
to dispose of the corpse in
an environmentally appropriate manner
like roadkill
then it will all be over
except for the shadow of a bloodstain
and I can grow old and bitter
without love getting in my way
anymore.

THIN WALLS

I don't hear toilets flushing,
couples arguing late at night,
televisions blaring alleged realities,
barking of dogs, screeching of parrots,
beds squeaking beneath lovers.

I don't hear car horns blaring,
busses farting, truck brakes squealing,
hookers yelling, or drunks wailing.

Going out of my door I don't
have to step over junkies nodding out,
or around puddles of urine,
or through piles of trash.

The thin walls of my home admit owls
hooting in the pre-dawn darkness,
horny foxes bragging their availability,
the occasional passing pickup truck,
the creaking of an old oak tree in the wind,
acorns hitting the sheet metal shed roof.

The sounds of my immediate world
neither frighten me nor cause me
to question my own humanity.

They soothe and assure me that
there is another reality beyond
urban degradation and humiliation
and, if I continue to be lucky, that
is where I will be able to stay.

THE OCCASIONAL UNACCOUNTABLE URGE TO CLEAN HOUSE

Periodically
even the spiders
must hope
that I will come
through and
clean house,
if only so they
can lay out
fresh webs –

A WALK THROUGH THE PAST

Walking around in memories
can be dangerous.

The ground of memory can be
soft, wet, sticky -
my feet sink into it -
it sucks off my shoes
leaving me barefoot
and shivering
in the steady rain of
what might have been.

The floors of memory are
brittle,
they shatter and splinter.
they give way
and I fall,
floor by floor, through a past
I no longer recognize and,
landing back where I began,
I understand even less.

TO BE HEARD

The rich man may speak softly,
politely, sound benevolent,
and still be heard
as he passes the cash
beneath the table -

The poor man must shout
and bang at the table
to be heard
not once
but over and over again
until the table shatters
and the machinations
of the rich are exposed,
the corruption made clear
the greed in their hearts
loosed at last to speak
louder
than their quiet, hollow
words would ever allow -

then will we be heard -

A FEW WEEKS BEFORE XMAS

The street people all seem to
emerge from culverts and fields
dragging shopping carts, backpacks
and improbable wheeled luggage
around the cold winter streets.
Neither begging nor panhandling.
Just moving. Shuffling along the
downtown sidewalks shaking the
last of clinging frost from their
old coats. Slipping through the
sharp sunlight between strings of
holiday lights and plastic wreaths
unnoticed among the shoppers and
sanitized xmas carols, which don't
need to be heard to inflict pain.

As though they are trying to recapture
something lost, something these other
people all seem to have, something
they may never have had in the first place
but are convinced they, at one time, did have.

Or maybe this poem
isn't about them at all.

PANHANDLED

1.
In street lamp twilight, in headlight flash -
at the mouth of the driveway of a discount
gourmet market, he stands. The hand-lettered,
cardboard sign held before him. A shield?
A mask? Such tired metaphors pile up -
it is a misplaced cartoon dialog balloon
and it boils down to:

hungry
can't find work

He looks to be in his mid-30's, bearded and
not at all bad looking - in fact I have always
preferred the scruffier types - and for
a moment I consider finding out how
hungry he may really be. What might he
be willing to do, or allow to be done to
him, to fill his belly? As I drive away,
his actual image already fading into the
sexual fantasy I'm concocting for us,
a question rises like a half-forgotten debt
dampening lust: When did I grow so cold?
What has brought me to this place
where another man's hunger incites
exploitation, rather than compassion?

So many years living with the gift of a
warm dry home, of an expanding belly, of
disposable income - as though I really had
control over such things. Knowing all the while
that I am two missed paychecks away from
spending each day with my own cardboard
sign at the bottom of a freeway exit ramp,
and my nights under some nearby bridge:
a shuffling, pleading, decaying drive-in movie
screen for the projected fantasies of passersby.

2. (1970)

Frank was good. Bold and unashamed. A natural at working the crowd and we, Jackie (his girlfriend), Jo (my girlfriend) and I, were the audience he played to. But this was not intended to be performance, it was a lesson and now, he indicated none too subtly, we were to go forth and do likewise. And we did. Spreading out among the mid-afternoon jostling of the downtown crowd in front of the Terminal Tower. Public Square. Cleveland. Busses and taxis and cars and pedestrian packed sidewalks. Everybody in transit of some kind, everybody moving - contact was fast and had to be established with as little fuss as possible. Frank's story about needing to bail his mother out of jail had been reduced to a few short phrases communicating the pathos of his fiction, without acknowledging its inherent ridiculousness. Frank was easily collecting twice as much as the three of us put together. And me, I got better at it as the summer went on.

  I wonder what those folks were thinking when they handed over their change? Did they believe we were destitute? Did any of them believe Frank's mother needed to be bailed out of jail? Did they see their own children? Or the children they had been? Did they see us at all?

  We were fresh out of a suburban high school. The money thus collected would go for gas, booze, and drugs.

  Later I would get good enough at panhandling to survive on it for short spells in cities like Boston and San Francisco. Eventually expanding into supermarket dumpster diving - that being in the days before dumpsters were padlocked to keep the garbage safe from trash like me.

3.
Thinking vaguely about the
parking meter I may need to
feed tomorrow, I draw a hand
out of my pocket, fist clenched
around 3 or 4 quarters, some
nickels and dimes, and pass
them to the man who has just
hit me up for spare change
on a sunny downtown street.

We had already passed each other.
I could have kept on walking.
It's not as though I'd actually
looked at him, or made eye contact.
Instead I stopped, imprecisely
weighed the change against
this morning's load of guilt,
and backed up to drop the
warm coins into his waiting
hand. Wondering if the debt
of my own panhandling days
might ever be paid in full -
and if so, what then?

ATTITUDE ADJUSTMENT

whatever passed for my positive
attitude is melting, dripping into
a puddle of paranoid negativity,
congealing on the floor at my feet,
hard to scrape off my shoes, hard to
walk away from without leaving
tracks which are much too easy
to follow, waiting for some sharp
toothed creature with a taste for
bad blood to pick up my trail and
drag me off into the darkness -
bitter meat for a desperate meal

PISSING IN THE SINK
(1976 - The Swiss American Hotel, San Francisco)

In this small hotel room the blue
and violet designs in the wallpaper,
meant to evoke flowers, seem to
crawl across the walls like picnic ants
over the sleeping body of a drunk.
The dresser is so close to the foot
of the bed I have to sit on the bed
to open the drawers all the way and
reach into the back for socks or
pornographic magazines from
the adult store down the street.
A chair crouches in the corner
between the narrow armoire
and the door like a thief stealing
space from the dirty carpet.
The night stand, a trapped pawn,
squeezes into the opposite corner.
On the other side of the
two windows the sink dribbles
nearly noiseless drops onto
rust stained porcelain.

But it is my own home now and
not the couch in someone else's

living room. Not an old school bus
abandoned in the front yard, nor
the floor of a spare room otherwise
full of boxed objects which will
never be unpacked until the person
dies and the heirs root through for
buried treasures from someone else's past.

And I can piss in the sink any time I want.

THE MAN ACROSS THE STREET

              used to beat his wife
in the middle of the night
in the middle of our dead-end street
      in the rain
      in the fog
      in the moonlight
      in cold sunlight
but he doesn't beat her anymore
            she's left him

the man across the street would
scream at his kids, and I was sure he
      beat them too
the look in their eyes, their
      slouched, wincing posture
old hound dogs crawling out from
under dead rusty pick-up trucks while
the father screams random drunken curses -
      they are gone now, too
- the kids

my roommate developed a strong
erotic attraction to the man across the street -
they never met, but the roommate would
watch him from behind the sheer fabric

of my aging curtains - would ooo and ahh while
talking to me, excited by the angry man's
taut-muscled, well-defined torso,
    the broad shoulders,
        strong arms and
     especially
  his tight
 compact
ass
roommate was no slouch in the
  torso and ass department
       himself
with youth on his side,
   fearless of folly -

  go ahead, I told him.
       we watched
as the man across the street,
   shirtless in the sun,
  loose beltless pants sliding down his
sweat-soaked butt, beer can
  gripped in his fist
     raged around his junk-strewn
obstacle course of a yard
       - aimless
  abandoned
   - all his animate targets gone
  left alone

without focus -

                go on over, I said,
        introduce yourself.

it is time.

SUBVERTING THE SUN

From 20 minutes' drive away
stiff ocean breezes cross the yard
subverting the warm sunlight.

The afternoon, like the morning,
casts a deep chill into my bones
as I stand outside the shadows

of the trees seeking sun warmth.
Some darkness inside me reaches out
to the cold rushing ocean air and

finds something recognizable within
its fleet frigidity and gripping me
from deep inside says, yes. Yes, yes.

THE BALLOONS ARE BACK

Though no one seems to have
notified the steamy afternoons,
these mornings know that
winter waits patiently
just down the way.

Three hot air balloons
float through the cold air of
a clear morning sky
until their baskets bump
the low brush of a dry meadow.
Then, with an immense sigh,
they stretch out across the dry grass
exhausted from the effort
of flight

INSOMNIA

God has no time for insomniacs, A.D. Winans,

Drugs take care of getting to sleep
but they don't last long enough.
The night rousts me
in the early morning hours with
its silence, its stillness, its emptiness.
This groggy mind eager to
be filled with random fears,
non-specific anxieties.
The loud beating of my own heart
within its glued-together chest,
sternum wired shut over re-inflated lungs,
bypassed arteries forever feeling left out.

In a restless bed the sheets shed splinters.
No position leads back to oblivion.
The ancient gods of sleep, Somnus and Hypnos,
ignore all entreaties no matter how desperate.
While the gods of the Christians and Jews
advise me to appreciate my
suffering sleeplessness
and be grateful for what it teaches.
But what does it teach?
Scrambled thoughts fighting
for dominance in a paranoid fog.

FOREST DREAMS

When a persistent wind tugs at its branches
does a redwood dream of wandering?

If a forest dreams would it dream of
becoming a multitude of coffins,
or houses, or rocking horses,
or chopsticks, or barstools,
or the skeletons of wingback chairs?

Or is that their nightmare?
Do trees have nightmares?

Do trees dream of lying quietly
on the forest floor gathering mosses
and slowly returning to the soil?
Or of being a bird lighting off from a branch, or
a gopher digging its way toward succulent roots?

Thirsty after four years of drought,
does a forest dream of becoming fire
and ascending into the sky as smoke?

Do a tree's dreams reside in
the farthest stretch of branch?
Or in the deepest reach of root?

Or do they arise from the heartwood
at the center of all circles
where youth echoes endlessly
through the years to vibrate
each needle and leaf to life?

HER BREATHING
(in memoriam LKS, 06/28/1948-05/04/2004)

Five labored breaths,
a pause after the fourth,
then silence -
then five more
and
then the silence
which
grows so long that
each time
i am afraid
she will not
ever
breathe
again -

and then
she
does

sometimes i hear
her voice when
she exhales -
the sound a
shadow makes
when it moves -
no words, just

the voice -
so familiar i know it
even like this

i wish i knew if she heard -
i tell her stupid things
that i've meant to say
but never seemed to
get around to -
embarrassing things
about love
and admiration

soon i realize that
i am waiting for
her breathing to
stop, not continue -
i want her pain
to end
and being helpless
to change anything
i wish for the
only end
available

briefly i feel
more like
her executioner
than caregiver

each time - after
the five breaths -
when the long
pause begins

- a pause longer
than I can hold
my breath -

i am afraid that
i won't
hear
another one -
then,
just when i think
this is it
there is that
sharp intake
of breath
and
the pattern

repeats

throughout
the cold night
into a colder
dawn.

ANOTHER SUICIDE

another man carries my mere
thoughts into movement, not

even desire articulated - shades
speculation and dubious comfort

now made certain by his action,
the distant final act of another -

this one dead, another gone,
and the hushed discussion

of when, where and how -
my cringing into cowardice

the whispered, *don't tell.*
please don't tell the others.

GRIEF

Grief has entered my heart.
it is trying to stake a claim there.
As though my heart were a
favored spot for panning gold,
or a prime piece of homestead
material, maybe with river
frontage and a good, cold well.

Grief has moved into my heart.
It has set up housekeeping there.
It is adding on rooms and
buying overstuffed used furniture,
making itself comfortable.
It appears to be planning
to stay for a long time.

Grief has become inseparable
from my heart, it lives here now.
It has no intention of ever leaving
and I am no longer able to imagine
my life without grief. It is
dug in and immovable like a
splinter that never grows out.

REMINDERS

In memoriam Paul Schwartz
(07/04/1966-01/27/2006)

dusty ocean sunset - colors
from a faded New Mexico desert
impatient sea gnashing its teeth
against the shore

do I grieve for the loss of my friend?
or the reminder of my own mortality?

this low-key pacific sunset
        burnt orange and
        pale ochre smear
        to powder blue -
beautiful, even without the
drama of blood soaked clouds
and heavenly shafts of golden light

the last thing a good
friend has to give -
                a reminder:
the simple joy in living -

horizon blushing its last,
darkness spreads

over the sea -

    turning around

moonlight.

GHOSTS IN THE MIST

A cold, dense morning mist
makes an ethereal graveyard
out of the neighboring vineyard

Ghosts lurk among grape stakes
drift above ground still wet
from rain several days ago

Find their way into the
photographs on my walls
trying to catch my eye

To lodge themselves within
my hollowed-out heart and fill it
with images and memories

Of a time when my dead friends
did not outnumber the living ones
and we thought that would last forever

REINVENTING THE DEAD

Sometimes I have the face
but the name is lost or
I'll have a nickname but
reach and scratch for the
birth name with no luck

Other times I have a name
but stumble around my memory
digging to unearth the face
to which it belongs

I am no longer remembering the dead
I am re-creating them,
reinventing them for
my own purposes
drawing out their nobility
accenting their evil
increasing their affection
redefining our relationship
until it meets my current needs
and they are not here
to get in the way
they aren't here to prove me wrong
they can no longer disappoint me,
shame me, best me, please me
they can no longer love me

and it is no longer them
who I love
it is my image of them
assembled from the memories that remain,
the objects, photographs, notes and letters
which carry them with me into
the balance of my days.

WALT WHITMAN POSES FOR BEAR MAGAZINE (1996)

It wasn't as though he'd never
posed for photographs before.
He enjoyed having his picture taken.
Matthew Brady shot a number of portraits.
It wasn't even like he'd never posed nude before.
Thomas Eakins shot a series of nude studies
and he had no problem with that.
But this felt a little different.

Don't worry, it's not just about your dick,
the photographer says to the Bard.
*It's about a body type and you
embody the type. So don't worry.
Still
we will need at least one good
boner shot
and one good butt shot –
you alright with that?*

The poet nods his head in the affirmative,
then, though hesitant, removes his clothes.
He hands them to Peter Doyle who, folding
them carefully, places them on a chair.
Doyle will also do the fluffing, if necessary.

Whitman is hoping for the cover,
it might help move some books:
poetry can be such a hard sell.

WALT WHITMAN ATTENDS A BEAR WEEKEND (2012)

I: AT THE POOL

"An unseen hand also pass'd over their bodies" – Song of Myself #11

Under an umbrella at a wrought metal poolside table
the Bard holds court in the dry August heat.
He wears a baggy swimsuit and Hawaiian shirt,
his now button bursting belly resting in his lap.
Peter Doyle sits beside him, attentive, protective.
It's been many years since the magazine spread
but his fans are loyal and there are new ones all the time
as old copies of the magazine circulate among younger readers
and his digitized image frequently turns up
on internet searches for bear.

He watches as men of all types and ages
splash in the cool water or float on
air mattresses in the amplified sunlight.
His eyes linger as they get in and out of the pool,
walk, talk, drink, flirt, glance over at him.
Most have some claim to being bears but
others are clearly chasers, bear hunters.
To him they are each beautiful in their own way.
He allows his eyes to caress them
as they pass before him; makes mental notes
for the poems he hopes will come later.
He thinks of how much his friend Tom Eakins
would have enjoyed all the men gathered
around the water, how he might have painted them.

Someone told me you're a famous poet.
One of them says to him.
Yeah, I heard that too, says another.
Recite a poem for us.
A book is drawn out of someone's bag
and handed to him. He leafs through.
Thinking again of Eakins, Whitman begins:
Twenty-eight young men bathe by the shore...

II: BEYOND THE BONFIRE
"I believe in the flesh and the appetites" – Song of Myself #24

In the transfiguring moonlight
Whitman finds himself on a dark trail
beyond the bonfire.
Here men who haven't hooked up
all day line both sides of the passage
considering their dwindling options.
Many have their trousers open,
shirts spread in the chill night,
trying to determine who will do
for the moment to slack the lust
grown deep throughout the day.

Peter Doyle had connected with a
handsome man late in the afternoon,
disappearing with him into one of the
corners of the small town.
Whitman will find him later, when
he returns alone to their rented bed.

For now he slowly moves down the trail,
his inquiring hand passing over the bodies,
the chests and bellies of the men as presented.
Reaching to stroke a bearded cheek or chin.
Brushing exposed crotches,

sometimes grasping, squeezing firmly
with a masculine grip, what he finds there.
Making eye contact whenever he can.

Pausing, Whitman takes it all in,
weighing both import and triviality.
He smiles into the shadows.
Another man stops in front of him,
looks into his eyes, finds invitation,
unbuttons the Bard's fly and
drops to his knees.
Whitman surrenders to the night.

CRUCIFIXIONS ARE BORING

The same tired old shtick for 2000 years -
Let's have a bloody beheading for a change,
Like they do to journalists in the Middle East -
Or how about throwing a savior off the top of a building
Like they do to the faggots in Saudi Arabia?
We could have a good old fashioned lynching with
Burgers flame broiled under a burning cross-
Or death by machete in the African style -

A savior could always be tied to the back of a
Pickup truck and dragged halfway across Texas -
There are so many possibilities, why limit ourselves?
Just read the newspapers, look at the online feed -
I'm sure if we give it some thought we can
Come up with a new way to dispose of a savior,
After all we are well-educated, creative people
Nothing holds us back except our imagination.

LOVING HUMANITY

is much easier from a distance

than in the
stifling air of a packed and
cramped commuter train

pushed and squeezed while
trying to remain standing
the coughers
the sneezers
muscles tensed with the
effort of staying upright
while the train lurches and
jerks doing its best to
dislodge you
trying not to touch anyone
not to elicit an
almost-under-the-breath
asshole
from another traveler

there is little room
for noble intentions
on a commuter train

it is easier to love
humanity
from a distance,
when you don't
have to deal
with people

FAILURE AS AN ADULT

Advancing into my late 60s
I don't own real property.
I don't have a retirement plan.
I have never married.
I have no children.

I have spent my life crafting words
almost nobody reads or hears.
Instead of accumulating money
I searched out experience.
Instead of securing a future
I tried to live each moment in the present.

And now the adults among my friends
are retiring, or planning on it,
secure in the homes they own,
budgeting for the income they will have,
some of them with Harleys
and vacation cabins.

They travel to exotic places
to skin dive or climb mountains
or just lie on foreign beaches
sipping cocktails that reflect
their locale as surely as

the ocean reflects the sunset
stretched across their horizon.

Meanwhile, with words and images,
I explore the possibilities and
fauna in my rented yard -
the feral black cat,
deer eating the loquat leaves,
raccoon tracks in the driveway,
fox scat on the front porch,
a dead rat at my back door.

THE RAINBOW AUGURY

Some odd sense of importance,
as though there were something
more than what is seen. This
need to detect in the music of chance
a composers hand, a logic.
Lessons from the movement
of objects, or their stasis.
Images or events, lingering
in the mind gathering with time,
meaning - like mold, like dust.

Is the air above a river wetter
than that above a meadow, a road?
Does it hold moisture and flow as the
water does below? Is the sky a river's
attic, full of algaed memories, and always
on the verge of sprouting rainbows?

Several miles east of Petrolia,
in the Mattole Valley,
a large rainbow stretches through the
narrow space between ridges,
poised lightly above the river.
There is no rain.
There had been no rain since the day before.

The sky is clear, faint wisps of cloud
hang in the corners like cobwebs,
and this rainbow, suspended
in the bright light,
its feet fading away
just before they
might have touched
the ground.

THE POLITICAL CLIMATE HEATS UP

Angry white people fulminate, rail,
and rage across the American landscape,
sporting T-shirts and baseball caps
bearing inflammatory slogans
and product endorsements.
Waving rifles and shaking fists.
Frightened that they may have
been left out of something but
they don't seem to know what it is.
So they attack those they think
have it and won't part with any.
Meanwhile the men who do
have everything, the obscenely
rich men, the powerful men,
pull everyone else's strings
pitting each against the other,
one ethnicity against another,
rural against urban,
zealots against atheists,
blue collar against white collar,
south against north,
the landlocked against the coasts,
high school dropouts against post-graduates -
everything except the one truth
hiding among them all:
it's the rich against the rest of us.

Bloated billionaires buy and sell
politicians, bribing them to bloviate
and spout obfuscating bafflegab
to distract attention from them
while they wallow in the endless
stream of money flowing their way
from government coffers and the
pockets and paychecks of the poor -
always plotting to acquire more.
And they laugh, confident that
they have missed nothing as they
relax on their luxury golf courses
sipping their gold-plated cocktails,
groping whomever they choose,
while mobs of angry white people
take to the streets to cheer them on.

MARCUS CONSIDERS A DOG

A fairly large one, he thinks,
indolent by nature, stationary.
Not some miniature breed
bouncing off the walls,
needing constant attention,
yapping, yapping, yapping.

And not one always wanting to chase balls,
digging up the small yard,
tracking in mud,
barking at birds,
howling with distant sirens,
chewing up shoes,
needing to be constantly petted and fed.
Not that kind of attention sucking
black hole of a dog at all.

And not a St. Bernard, Sheepdog, or Samoyed
it must be one that doesn't shed
or need to be barbered and bathed too often;
nothing requiring frequent elaborate grooming.

And nothing that stares at him when he eats,
drooling from a droopy, pathetic face.
Not one that begs at all.

He wants one that blends into his environment
there, but out of the way until called on for
comfort, conversation, companionship;
grateful for food and a place to live.
A contented creature, self-contained,
happy to spend time by himself until
called on to be man's best friend.
That's the kind of dog Marcus wants.
He is open to suggestions.

THE ABSENCE OF BIRDS

Bare tree in a field of snow.
Dead tree,
three thick shafts,
broken, the arms
that would reach the sun
broken, undone.
No bud in spring.
No leaf in lazy summer.
No bright burst of autumn blood.
It stands alone
amid the frozen swamp land,
the high water weeds,
the icy eggs of frog.

IN DECEMBER WOODS

deer and dog
tracks frozen in
the mud crunching
beneath my boots

brittle black shale
on the steep path

bare trees creaking
in the wind

a not-so-distant
echo of rifle fire

iron water in the
blood-red creek bed

A SLOW COLLAPSE

As though hesitant to
lie down at last
the old garage leans
precariously to the south
holding still in mid-collapse
occasionally shedding asphalt
shingles like lizard scales
like blue jay feathers lying
on the overgrown grass

An early morning fog
covers the old garage
like a pale ink wash
over a careful sketch
obscuring the details while
thickening the mood

The door hangs open,
a gaping, puzzled mouth,
I left it that way yesterday
when I decided I'd mown
enough yard for one day
and simply stopped, leaving
the mower where it sat and
the garage open to invasion by
all manner of nocturnal critters

rummaging about its contents
not caring that it leans
and one day will crash to
the ground in slow motion
lying still at last waiting to
be absorbed into the earth
sinking beneath the surface
and held there to become coal,
diamond, petrified wood
eventually easing
back up through the dirt
toward the surface and sunlight
millennia from now
as something precious.

MOONLIGHT & MUSIC

Skeleton shadows reach across the damp winter night driven by the near-glacial movement of moonlight through the trees. They quiver on blades of grass which shift slowly in a barely perceptible breeze. The man, whose sole purpose in standing in this yard at this moment had been to piss, hears, as though from the subtle scratching of bare branches above his head, a precise interaction of strings. The final Shostakovich quartet, the fifteen, creeping from out the open back door, one adagio doggedly stalking another through the crisp air, companion to the barely slithering shadows of the naked trees. As though each note had been carved out of the night sky by the calculated wielding of sharp-edged stars then laid upon the man in layers of chilled moonlight-infused, funereal filigree, beautiful to the eye but incapable of warmth.

The man shivers from head to toe, zips up and goes back inside.

THE BELT

We moved to Bennington St.
when I was 8 years old and,
once settled in there, the Belt
took up permanent residence in
the hall linen closet, warm and
comfortable among sheets and
towels and wash cloths. Worn
brown leather, buckle missing,
removed so no real harm
would be done.

In secret I would open the
closet, thread a hand in among
the linen until I could feel the
sacred object hidden away
when not in use, like the wine
and chalice at church. Petting
it with fingertips, a creature whose
unstable nature leaves open the
possibility of losing fingers poked
cavalierly into its cage.

The mood of each whippin' would
be established by whether dad
coldly told me to go get the Belt
and bring it to him, in which case

the whipping would be grounded
with a clear lesson learnin' approach
fighting back fear, or my own anger,
or whether he, with the passionate
impatience of rage, went for it himself.
Then I would lose my own anger in the
face of such rage and by the time he
would return, one end of the Belt
wrapped around his hand, the other end
gripped tightly in the same hand, I
would be in tears, broken simply by
his rage, his words: *You think you got
something to cry about, boy? I'll
give you something to cry about.*
And then he would.

SNAP

every now and then, when i'm home, undressing after work,
removing my office drag, replacing it with something more
real, every now and then I unbuckle my belt and, grabbing
the buckle firmly, yank it quick as i can through the loops so it
makes the snapping sound that used to so terrify me as a child -

back then this not only meant that I was about to get a whipping
but, because my father was not using the linen closet belt and
instead was taking off his own to do it, the swiftness with which
he pulled it, the sharp snap as it passed through each loop told
me he was really angry and this one was going to hurt -

now I'm over 60 and I do it, startled to realize that the sound
brings him back in ways a photograph cannot and it is not fear that
I feel nor hatred for the man who beat me - it is a longing affection,
an odd reminder perhaps that one of the few times we ever touched
was when he would hold me while he beat me with his belt -

MY FATHER'S POST-MORTEM APOLOGY

To wake, with *Gayne's Adagio*
seeping out of the radio, pretending
to be an alarm, and expecting to feel
tears sliding out of a dream and down
my face, a wet and rumpled pillowcase,
my father's unexpected embrace.

Lingering in the air around me are
benevolent fireflies, minuscule
guardian angels, ghosts formed from
the words of my father's apology,
his earnest request for forgiveness,
his protestations of love.

But in this cold morning half-light
there are no tears on my pillow and
his words remain locked in a dream
to which access has been denied,
all memory of how they got here
fading into daylight consciousness
leaving me to ponder the stagnant
list of my own apologies remaining
unsaid to the living and to the dead.

WHAT THE NIGHT KEEPS
"the night / always keeps something" – Kent Taylor

the unguarded
hours
offered
in hope of
appeasement

fears that pass
with the dawn

dry tears
empty sighs
stifled screams

secrets
generated
by dreams

demons
and
gods

the poem
composed
in my
fading mind

in those
wakeful
ticking
minutes
lying
alone
in the
dark

THE FUTURE

For my mother

i was not your dreams come to life
i was never meant to be

i was a spark shot out of your youth
intended to ignite the future

and now, my own youth moving further
away with every minute, i assure you
i am not your failure sent to haunt you -

my light may grow dimmer by the day
and the future sure ain't what it used to be
but some spark remains and as long as it does

i will burn toward tomorrow
and the past be damned

STOCKS OPEN UP

Bad news fills the enveloping aether,
the smoke and ash of misinformation
clogging the air so it is hard to breathe,
clogging the mind so it is hard to think.
Minor members of the plutocracy panic.
Politicians trip over themselves turning
on each other trying to escape scandal.
Wars, promulgated for profit, fought
by desperate volunteers, mercenaries,
and zealots continue to rage and burn
around the globe in distant places
too easy to marginalize and forget.
The price of everything increases.
Tax cuts for corporations trickle down as
increased charges for the rest of us -
money for that bloated military budget
has to come from somewhere.
Hurricanes flood out communities.
Wildfires burn out neighborhoods.
But everything is okay this morning
because stocks have opened UP.
There are profits to be made from misery
so stocks have opened UP.
Disaster turns easily to dollars
so stocks have opened UP.

Scandal transmutes into entertainment
so stocks have opened UP.
There are new records to be broken
now that stocks have opened UP.
And I sit here with my little IRA,
tugging at the tuxedo coattails
of profiteers, pillagers, and philanderers,
counting the incremental increase in
my pale, inadequate retirement fund.
Wondering how I ever allowed myself
to be leveraged into this system,
to profit from this evil in even so small
a way and how I could ever survive
into old age without its meager
payoff for my tacit collaboration.

THE NORCO KICKS IN

Waking in the night,
the day's sticky heat barely
disguised by the cold night air
this fan drags unwilling
through the window.

Pain hovers just at the point of
discomfort,
       no wincing, no moaning
just this nocturnal restlessness.

I can almost touch sleep.

QUIT: DAY 11

    at a loss,
    our hero
    keeps trying to
                find
    something to do
    w/his hands,
         empty now
         of cigarettes
    they seem
    oddly idle
    and obvious
                like
    ten
    sore
    thumbs.

IMPULSE

Standing in line at the market
idly checking out the impulse items
carefully placed on display there.
One last chance for corporate hands
to slip into my wallet before
I pay for my goods and leave.

There, among the marshmallow
critters on sticks, tabloid papers,
butane lighters and breath mints
are racks of little liquor bottles:
neatly arranged in rows, dust free,
attractively packaged and so convenient.

The old familiars are still there,
as though mentoring the upstart brands.
I note that there are now enough flavors of
schnapps and vodka to make Howard Johnson
himself turn green with envy. Not even a
wooden case of 24 Nehi sodas sitting beneath
the grape arbor to keep cool on a
hot summer's day could offer so many
colors and varieties of sticky sweet
liquid to catch the light and
thereby the eye. But those are
easy to resist, I'd stopped playing

with such confections fairly early,
relegating them to Christmas stockings
and other people's birthday parties.

It is the half-pint, pocket size
bottles of bourbon that cause
my arm to impulsively twitch
as though about to shake the
hand of an old friend, long gone
but now returned to my side.

On this day, if I had a button
to push to atomize all of humanity
I would push it, without hesitation -
thrust the entire useless mass of
us into the air, to scatter into
loose formations of drifting
lazy cloud and then rain
back down as something which
might have use in some way;
might nourish instead poison.

Yet even today my hand stays
at my side, stuck in a pocket,
fingering coins, pocket knife
and a small brass disc with a
roman numeral in the center
of one side.

RED FLAGS IN NOVEMBER

With no rain to speak of so far this year
fire warnings appear in November.

On the western edge of the Sierra
the Camp Fire bursts through Paradise,
consuming everything it encounters,
making its way down to the valley.
Acres of trees and buildings burning.
Smoke and ash drift on the wind
hundreds of miles west to darken
the coastal skies and thicken
the air with burnt bitterness.
White specks spotting my brown car
re-awaken memories best left
in the past, in the poems
engendered by last year's fires,
filed and almost forgotten.

What can we divine from this
latest massive sideromancy, these
grasses smoldering on overheated earth,
or the sickly orange light of morning
as the sun tries to burn through
cold smoke without success.
What is to be learned from this?

The transitory essence of everything?
The basic inhospitality of existence?
The whims of fate and weather?
Or simply the great appetite of fire
and the potential for everything else,
including you and me,
to be consumed within it.

AIR QUALITY INDEX

There has been no rain since
early October and the fires,
in different places this year,
are again having their way
with California as the year
creeps through November
without relief - the smoke
hanging undisturbed in the air.
Even here, over a hundred miles
away from the nearest blaze,
the air quality index tells me
to stay indoors all week and
through this weekend and
beyond until rain arrives.

Standing outside in the cold,
sickly yellow light of morning
I watch my breath condense
as the sun tries to burn through
what has already burned once
as though smoke were mere mist
to be dispersed by a warm day.

DISASTER PORN

Desperate for information
I turn on the TV news
and there it all is: maps, charts,
photographs, videos,
interviews with the victims
of this immense natural disaster,
these marauding wildfires

Frightened of errant embers
I hang on predictions
of wind speed and direction,
listen to meteorologists and
experts of all manner and
levels of expertise

Fire chiefs, police chiefs,
somber and careful
grant interviews
hold press conferences
speaking precisely while
firefighters and cops
caught between acts of
increasing heroism
toss off-the-cuff comments
toward the camera
assuring us all that our
lives are in capable hands.

Meanwhile, looters,
politicians, and grifters
are looking for an angle
to make hay from fire.

So I watch, absorbing each
scrap of information,
internalize shell-shocked
witness testimony,
listen to stories of loss,
abstractly exploring the limits of tragedy
and it all accumulates within me,
as I sit helpless, a watcher
an observer, not a participant
and grateful not to be
among those who know the depths
of the events happening over there,
on the other side of the county.

I search my address book memory,
where exactly does this friend live?
How close is that friend to the
advancing flames?
Why haven't I heard back from them?

And I keep watching the TV news
as it starts to repeat and repeat,
talking heads spouting the same words

the same charts, the same images,
the same carefully edited videos,
and each time I see the same victim
my heart aches again and I realize,
sitting in my safe and untouched home,
I'm feeling vicarious victimhood, a sense
of sharing in the experience of others
to which I have no real insight.
Still I keep watching the same things
over and over again, hanging on every
repeated word until I can almost
recite them myself from my perch
on the edge of an easy chair
in my comfortable home. But
I keep watching anyway,
masturbating my emotions
to an unanticipated pitch then
backing off, sated.

I turn off the TV,
take a pill,
climb into bed,
hope it will all be gone
in the morning.

THE FINCH

The finch I caught in the living room
lay still between my cupped hands,
no longer charging the unyielding window.

On the porch railing I gently rest my hands
then slowly uncap one from the other
until the finch sits there in the fleshy nest

of my palm, dormant as death. Then, looking
around in that jerky bird manner, it erupts
in a burst of feathers and flies across the yard.

From my perch on the porch I lose it in the trees,
examine the day in front of me, my place in it,
turn and return to the house, leaving the door open.

POEMS TRAVEL

postal vessels -
stark card or
folded in upon
themselves,
cradling text,
crossing the land,
hand to hand
to machines
with feet,
with wheels,
with wings and
back into hands
guided to
the right box
so far away

CLOCKS DON'T TICK

alarm clocks
don't tick
anymore
setting off
the time
second
by
second
tick
by
tock
stretching
across a
sleepless
night

instead their
numbers glow
in the darkness
gap-toothed
disembodied
digital grin
countdown to
morning
launch

into a day
already
cursed
and wasted
before I
even get
out of
bed

INDEPENDENCE DAY, 2018

(arranged by Christopher Franke)

This year it is
a new Independence Day,
a day on which
my country can celebrate:

Our independence
from logic, from reason, from truth,
from evidence, from scientific method,

Independence from facts, from integrity,
from morality, from ethics,
from decency,

Independence from the Constitution,
from legislative process, from treaties,
from comity, from culture,
from civility,

Independence from compassion,
from kindness, from charity,
from racial equality, from economic equality, from
gender equality.

Time truly to celebrate
our independence
from civilization!

So light the fireworks
& send them cascading
into the air, rank after rank,
to explode

in empty displays
of brief blinding light
& deafening roar

like giant guns going off
in the distance
of somebody else's war
achieving, in the end,
nothing more
than to frighten
the dogs and babies.

Pop open another beer,
crack the seal on that whisky,
as the grills cool down
in the chill night
& the speakers blast
nostalgic, patriotic songs
from a time when independence
meant more than a license to bully,
more than permission to piss on
anyone
who doesn't look and act like you.

TODAY, TOMORROW

The tediousness of each day
perpetuated and punctuated by
the same manufactured diversions
as the day before and the day after.
Mood flat, ambition dead or dormant,
nothing seems worth saying anymore.
Yesterdays of action grow more
distant and vague, details need
to be created to flesh out
memories - what did happen?
What really did happen?
Did any of it really happen?
Or have I always been floating,
suspended in an aspic of uncertainty,
indifference, and boredom?
Able to see out but not get out
until getting out no longer
matters and memory dissipates
along with everything else.

THE CURE FOR DEPRESSION

St. John's Wort blooming yellow
in the grey, overcast morning
as though it thought it could
cure an atmospheric depression.

After Emily Dickinson
("Split the Lark and you'll find the music" – E.D.)

Split a lark and the guts spill out,
What little there may be -
And if you should have any doubt
You can just check with me –

For I have split both mammal and bird,
As well as a reptile or two,
Finding but gore and blood and turd,
The same, each time I do –

In seeking the source of music,
Or beauty or grace of flight,
It will only serve to make you sick
To bring such things to light -

Singing arises from the spirit,
Not from the meat and the bone,
Listen closely whenever you hear it
And leave the source alone -

USED BOOK

paging through a new used book
of poetry, straightening out the
corners of pages folded over by a
previous owner marking, I presume,
favored poems or passages - I look
for a pattern, a link between the marked
pieces, a thread to follow to lead me to
the hand that previously held this book
the eyes that searched through pages for
just the right words, seeking a resonance
of image and idea echoing within
before finally, having gleaned all
there was for them to find,

they sold it

and now,
I hold it.

IN ORLANDO
(June 12, 2016)

Forty-nine of our brothers and sisters slain
And fifty-three more wounded
Sadness and grief hover
In the background, awaiting their turn
Right now it is the clenched fist
The tensed jaw of anger which
Is all I can and need to feel

The gunman's father makes excuses
Earlier in the day his son saw
Two men kissing in Miami
And maybe that set him off
Maybe that justifies his rampage

From acceptable to hate
To acceptable to exterminate
Is too short a step

In a month full of marches
Celebrating how far we have come
How much has been gained
This is a gut churning reminder
Of how much is yet to be done
How much further we have to go
To not be considered valid targets

Of hatred, fear, and bullets
Attack one of us, you attack us all
Kill one of us
And that violence echoes through us all
Ricocheting within our core
Taking up residence in our hearts

Still we will keep coming out
Keep fighting
Keep expressing our love
Openly and unapologetically
Until it is no longer acceptable to kill us
In Uganda or in New Delhi
In Saudi Arabia or in Orlando

THE LOST POEM

The poem slipped within the
    flannel sheets with me
making itself known in a brief
    moment of consciousness
between waking and drifting
    back to restless sleep -
then, like a faithless lover, it
    disappeared before morning,
leaving only a sense of loss and
    this poor substitute you're reading.

PARABLE OF THE END OF TIME

The sky fell off a roof, it lay on the
ground unconscious as the day darkened -
paramedics arrived in record time
using all their resuscitative powers -
the sky's eyes opened briefly,
admitting a quiescent twilight -
when the eyes closed again
near-total darkness returned -
they say the sky died in the ambulance
on the way to the hospital.

The earth trembled.
The sea wept.

In the darkness that ensued
the sea stumbled off a desert cliff
and crashed onto sharp rocks below -
the earth, unable to break the sea's fall,
felt the thud resound throughout its crust -
paramedics, lost in the dark, arrived too late to help -
the sea died on an obscure stretch of dry land.

Eventually the earth, alone and frightened,
spasmed and shivered from pole to pole, let out
one last great cry full of hurricanes and volcanos,
then it, too, died -

When the earth died there were many
rich men who never even noticed
until their wealth evaporated into
the cold nothing that remained -
and when they expired, along
with the rest of life on earth,
the expanding universe sighed once
before continuing on its way.

I SHOULD FALL IN LOVE AGAIN

Because it has been too long
because I've forgotten what it feels like
because I have curled up too far into myself
because winter is coming and every night grows colder
because too many of my friends are getting married
because I need a date for their weddings
because I can't keep living for myself alone
because I need to care for someone else
because my cat has been dead for four years
because I've forgotten why I swore off love
because I've always been a bit of a masochist
because I've always been a hopeless romantic
because I need a new kind of pain in my life
because I've grown to appreciate my own farts
because I need a reason to exercise and diet
because I need someone to cook for
because I cannot walk on the beach alone anymore
because I have curled up too far into myself
because I've forgotten what it feels like
because it has been too long since I've fallen in love.

NATURE BOY

    The boy showed me a tiny frog
    in a 3 pound coffee can with holes
                               in the lid.
    Told me of a giant salamander
               at the local swimming hole.
    Chased a small lizard, not much
         bigger than my thumbnail, around
               the asphalt, under the car door
                   and back.
             Caught it
  then
               popped it into his mouth
                   to see the look on my face.

I like snakes he said and told me of his further
        reptilian conquests.
We discussed tadpoles. Then, when my
        responses ceased to amuse him
he wandered off across the parking lot
until he was absorbed by the woods.

AS A CHILD

to see the world as a child
with the understanding of years.

each wonderful thing
wondering back
smiling
open to all facets of what it is
or was or could/would or might be.
each possibility.

as a child who
does not yet know what it all means
but
wants so to learn.

M.J. (Michael Joseph) Arcangelini was born 1952 in western Pennsylvania, grew up there & in Cleveland, Ohio. He's resided in northern California since 1979 and currently lives in Sonoma County. He began writing poetry at age 11. His work has been published in a lot of little magazines (including *The James White Review, White Crane Journal, Whisky Island, Taproot, ArtCrimes, Ev'ryman, Splitw*sky, RFD, BEAR Magazine, Jonathan, lilliput, Rusty Truck, The Ekphrastic Review, The Gasconade Review*) and over a dozen anthologies. He is the author of the full length collection *With Fingers at the Tips of My Words* (2002) from Beautiful Dreamer Press (http://www.beautifuldreamerpress.com/) and the chapbooks *Room Enough* (2016) and *Waiting for the Wind to Rise* (2018) both from Night Ballet Press (http://nightballetpress.blogspot.com/). A chapbook, *Pawning My Sins*, is scheduled for 2019 from NightBallet Press. He maintains an occasional blog with memoirs and poems at https://joearky.wordpress.com/ Arcangelini has been nominated for a Pushcart Prize.

www.ingramcontent.com/pod-product-compliance
Lightning Source LLC
Chambersburg PA
CBHW020124130526
44591CB00032B/523